THE ART OF SIGN LANGUAGE

PHRASES

THE ART OF SIGN LANGUAGE

PHRASES

Christopher Brown

THUNDER BAY
P·R·E·S·S

San Diego, California

Thunder Bay Press
An imprint of the Advantage Publishers Group
5880 Oberlin Drive, San Diego, CA 92121-4794
www.thunderbaybooks.com

Produced by PRC Publishing
The Chrysalis Building, Bramley Road, London W10 6SP, U.K.

An imprint of **Chrysalis** Books Group plc

ISBN 1-59223-090-3

Library of Congress Cataloging-in-Publication Data

Brown, Christopher, 1954–
        The art of sign language: phrases / Christopher Brown
        p. cm.
        ISBN 1-59223-090-3
1. Signed English. 2. Sign language—Phraseology. L Title.

HV2474.B772 2003
419'.7—dc21
2003050697

Printed and bound in Malaysia

3 4 5 07 06 05 04

The publisher wishes to thank Simon Clay for taking all the photography
in this book, including the cover photography.
Photography © PRC Publishing Limited 2003.
All enquiries about photography should be directed to Chrysalis Images.

Contents

Introduction

The Art of Sign Language: Phrases is a useful reference book that will benefit both people learning to sign and those who suddenly find they need to communicate with deaf people who sign. The format of the phrases and sentences used are easily adapted to incorporate other vocabulary.

The first book in the series, *The Art of Sign Language*, is the foundation for this book. It is the foundation upon which this is based and the chapters of this book have been arranged in a similar order to those of the first book. This second book shows how to form simple phrases using some of the vocabulary presented in the first book, as well as incorporating new vocabulary.

There are two forms of sign language that have evolved in North America, both sharing the same vocabulary. A.S.L. (American Sign Language) was originally developed to express whole thoughts or ideas, using a sentence structure that is different from written or spoken English. This is the format that is commonly used

where large amounts of information are to be expressed, as it is a much faster method of sign communication. However, for those of us who are accustomed to the syntax of spoken English, Signed English is much easier to grasp because it follows the familiar word order that we are used to. The Signed English format, therefore, is used throughout this book in order to help the novice signer.

It must be remembered, however, that apart from the use of the signs contained in this book, all sign language is only one part of a communication tool. Whenever Signed English is used, English is spoken simultaneously and slightly exaggerated body language is used to emphasize feelings and emotions.

As with all spoken languages in current use, sign language continues to evolve, change, and adapt to the needs of the world in which it is used. Even in the short period since the publication of *The Art of Sign Language*, some signs may have changed and new ones evolved. The signs that are used in this book are current at the time of publication, but do not be surprised to find that some of the signs are not in current usage. Another factor to consider is regional variation. In the same way that spoken words may vary in different parts of a country, with each regional variation being equally correct, so there are such regional variations with the use of sign language. In this book, the most commonly used sign for an idea has been presented, and chances are that this will be universally understood, even if it is not the preferred sign in a particular region.

CREATION OF PHRASES

Remember the golden rule with signing: It is impossible for everyone to know every sign; indeed, there are some words that do not have their own sign. If you cannot find a sign for something, or if you have simply forgotten the sign (this is human and excusable), then finger spelling can help you out of this situation. Even experienced signers will resort to finger spelling under these circumstances, so do not be afraid to use this method.

Although Signed English follows the pattern of the spoken word, there are certain nuances that are not reflected in the sign itself. When a part of speech is changed, the basic sign remains the same. For example, the sign for the word "quick," an adjective, will be the same as the sign for the word "quickly," an adverb. To reflect this, a sign marker will be added after the sign itself. Sign markers are also used in other contexts; for example, although all basic verb signs are in the present tense, a marker would be used to express future or past.

Similarly, an agent/person marker is used to change a verb into a noun indicating the person or thing that fulfills that function. For example, the verbs "clean," "work," and "drive" would become "cleaner," "worker," and "driver." (This marker is shown by placing both palms inward at chest level and lowering them slowly and simultaneously along the line of the body.)

Having referred to these tools that are used to make Signed English reflect the nuances of the spoken language, people using the language have to make certain decisions as to how much these tools are used in this form of communication. It must not be forgotten that, as with other forms of sign language, Signed English is not only comprised of signs, but also the use of body language and a spoken mouth pattern. The "receiver" then not only understands what is meant by observing the signs used, but also the mouth pattern and body language of the signer. When communicating with a child, who is perhaps not as proficient at receiving sign language, it is important to employ all three of these tools to enhance his understanding. However, in everyday conversational use, it is more common for sign and agent markers to be omitted, since their use slows the communication process and the shades of meaning expressed by them are readily obvious from the context of the sentence and because of the lip pattern of the signer.

Most of these additional tools are omitted here, as this book is intended to be a guide that is easy to use for someone who is trying to achieve a basic grasp of Signed English. It is mainly written to enable the user to establish some level of conversation in an everyday situation. Communication with deaf children requires special attention, for which special publications are available. The abbreviations used in the written explanation of the signs are in exactly the same format as in *The Art of Sign Language*. The only true abbreviations used are self-explanatory: L for left and R for right. To avoid the reader having to be aware of formal hand shapes, alphabetic letters are used to explain the hand shape for the novice reader. For example, the explanation for "aunt" reads: "R 'A' sign palm out, wiggle at side of R cheek." The way to interpret this would be, "Sign the letter 'A' with the right hand, with the palm facing outward. Having formed the hand shape in this way, wiggle it at the side of the right cheek."

Alphabet

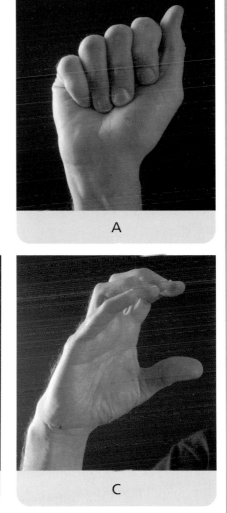

A

B

C

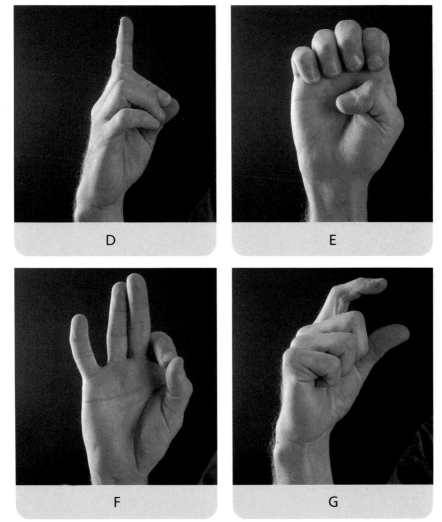

D

E

F

G

Alphabet H–J

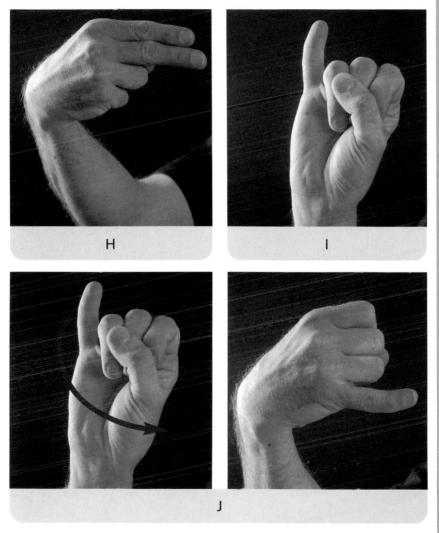

H

I

J

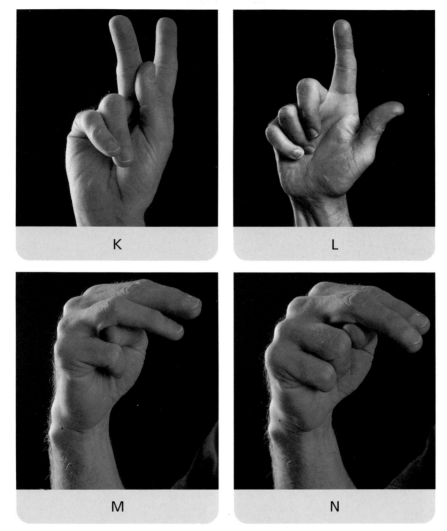

K

L

M

N

Alphabet O–R

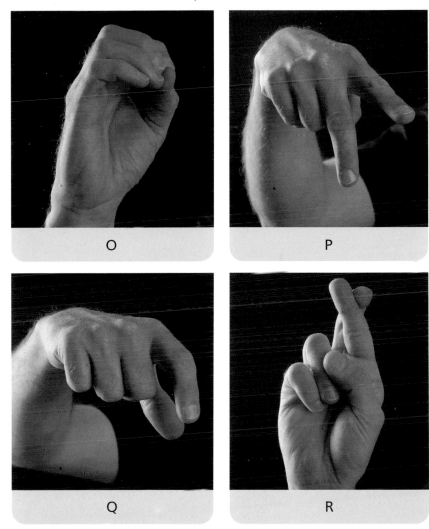

O

P

Q

R

ALPHABET

13

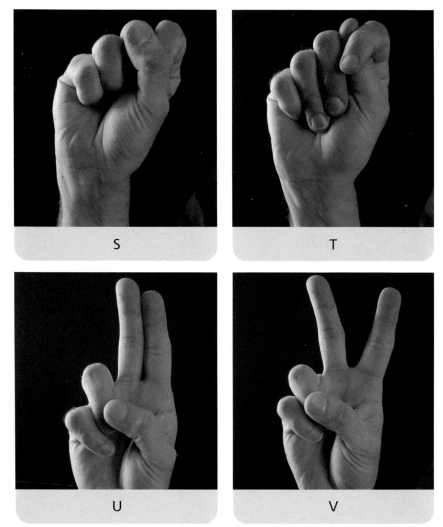

S

T

U

V

Alphabet W–Z

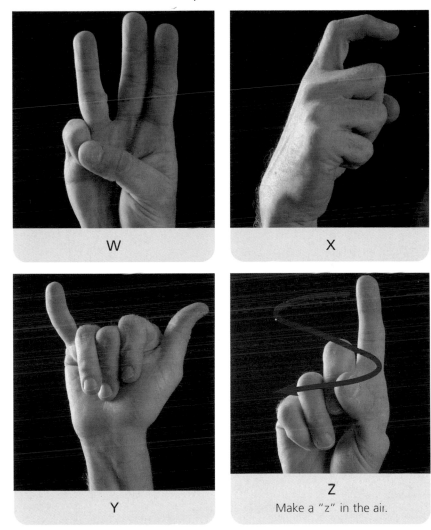

W

X

Y

Z
Make a "z" in the air.

Good afternoon/morning.

Useful
Phrases

GOOD
Touch lips with fingers of R hand, move forward into upturned palm of L hand.

AFTERNOON

L arm in front of body, palm down, pointing R. R forearm, palm down, resting on back of L hand, pointing slightly upward.

MORNING

Place fingertips of R hand in crook of L arm. Raise L arm, palm up, to vertical position.

How are you?

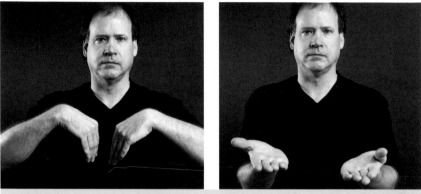

HOW
Curved hands back to back, fingers pointing down. Rotate hands inward, turning fingers up.

ARE
"R" sign from chin, moving forward.

YOU
Point R index finger at subject.

?
Form question mark in the air with R index finger.

I'm OK, thank you.

OK
Finger spell "O" and "K."

THANK YOU
Place fingertips of R hand against mouth and move forward.

Please/You're welcome.

PLEASE
Rub chest in circular motion.

YOU'RE WELCOME
Place fingertips of R hand against mouth and move forward in an arc.

My name is . . .

MY
Tap chest with R hand.

NAME
Place middle finger of R "H" across index finger of L "H."

IS
Place little finger of R hand against chin and move it forward.

[NAME]
Finger spell your name

What is your name?

WHAT
Draw tip of R index finger down L palm, palm facing inward.

IS
Place little finger of R hand against chin and move it forward.

YOUR
Point R palm forward.

NAME
Place middle finger of R "H" across index finger of L "H."

?
Form question mark in the air with R index finger.

23

What is the time?

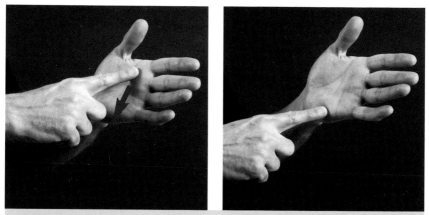

WHAT
Draw tip of R index finger down L palm, palm facing inward.

IS
Place little finger of R hand against chin and move it forward.

TIME
Tap wrist.

?
Form question mark in the air with R index finger.

Where is the hospital?

WHERE
R index finger up, palm out.
Shake back and forth.

IS
Place little finger of R hand
against chin and move it forward.

HOSPITAL
With R "H," draw small cross on
L upper arm

?
Form question mark in the air
with R index finger.

Who is your friend?

WHO
Circle R index finger in front of lips.

IS
Place little finger of R hand against chin and move it forward.

YOUR
Point R palm forward.

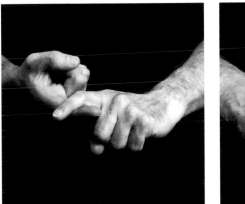

FRIEND
Hook L index finger over R, which is palm up. Reverse.

?
Form question mark in the air with R index finger.

When is your birthday?

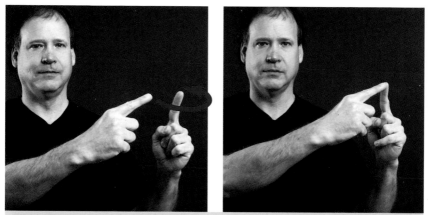

WHEN
Circle L index finger with R index finger, then touch tips of index fingers.

IS
Place little finger of R hand against chin and move it forward.

YOUR
Point R palm forward.

BIRTHDAY

L palm down, pointing to R. Back of R hand under L palm, move forward.

Point R index finger up, point L hand to R elbow, and pivot R arm down to L elbow.

?

Form question mark in the air with R index finger.

29

My husband has an appointment at the dentist.

People

MY
Place open palm on chest.

HUSBAND
Mime grabbing brim of a hat with R forefingers and thumb.

Clasp extended L hand with palm up.

HAS
Place fingertips of both hands against the chest.

APPOINTMENT
Circle R "A" hand above L "S" hand, which is pointing right. Touch wrists.

DENTIST
Tap right side of mouth with R "D."

The doctor is a friend of my son.

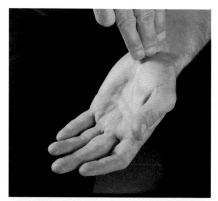

DOCTOR

Flat L hand palm up, tips out, tap L wrist with fingertips of R "M."

IS

Place little finger of R hand against chin and move it forward.

FRIEND

Hook L index finger over R index finger and reverse.

MY
Place open palm on chest.

SON
Mime grabbing brim of a hat with R forefingers and thumb.

Place R hand palm up in crook of L arm.

I have three children, two boys and one girl.

I
R "I" hand on chest.

HAVE
Place fingertips of both hands against the chest.

THREE
Hold up thumb and index and middle fingers, palm out.

CHILDREN
Lower R hand, palm down, as if indicating a small child, then bounce to right.

TWO
Hold up index and middle fingers, palm out.

  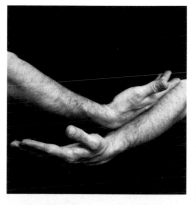

BOYS

Mime grabbing brim of hat with R forefingers.

Place R hand, palm up, in crook of L arm.

ONE

Hold up index finger.

GIRL

Draw line with R thumb along cheek.

Place R hand, palm up, in crook of L arm.

Our aunt is coming to visit.

OUR

R "D" against R side of chest, arc around to L side of chest.

AUNT

R "A," palm out, wiggle at side of R cheek.

IS

Place little finger of R hand against chin and move it forward.

COME

"1" sign both hands, palms up, tips out. Bring tips up and back toward chest.

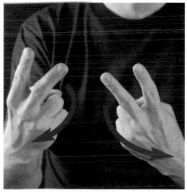

VISIT

"V" sign both hands, palms in, circle away from the body.

That brother and sister are twins.

THAT
Place R "Y" on
upturned L palm.

BROTHER
Mime grabbing brim of hat with R forefingers.

Tap index fingers
together, palms
down and tips out.

SISTER
Draw line with R thumb along cheek.

Tap both index fingers together, palms down and tips out.

TWINS
Place R "T" sign on L side of chin, then on R.

ARE
Place tip or R "R" against chin and move forward.

Please ask his wife's name.

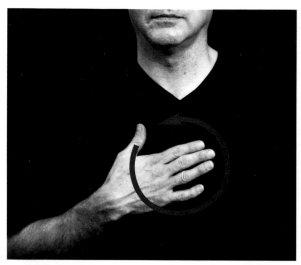

PLEASE
Rub open hand in a circle against chest.

ASK
Place open hands together and draw toward the body.

HIS
R palm out and pushed toward subject.

WIFE
Descend R thumb down R cheek.

Clasp hands together.

NAME
Tap middle finger of R "H" on index finger of L "H."

Her parents are old.

HER
R palm out and
pushed toward
subject.

PARENTS
R "P" sign, place middle finger on R side of forehead, then on cheek.

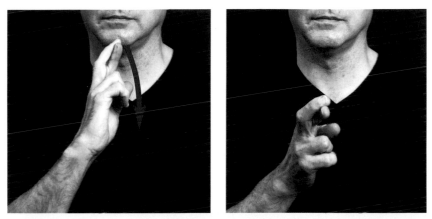

ARE

Place tip of R "R" against chin and move forward.

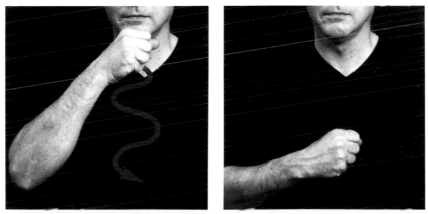

OLD

R "S" grabs fictitious beard at chin and moves down in wiggling motion.

The nurse's nephew and niece are family friends.

NURSE
Flat L hand, palm up, tips out, tap L wrist with fingertips of R "N" twice.

NEPHEW
R "N," wiggle at R temple.

NIECE
R "N," wiggle at R jawline.

ARE
Place tip of R "R" at chin and move forward.

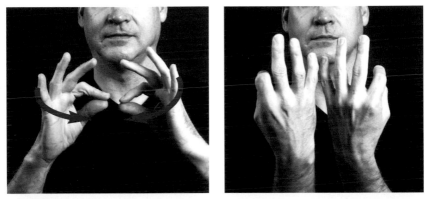

FAMILY

R and L "F," palms out and index fingers touching, draw around and apart until little fingers touch.

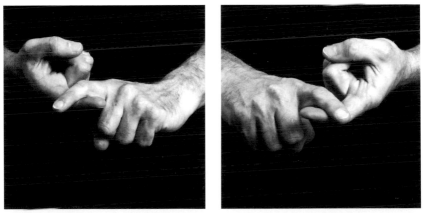

FRIENDS

Hook L index finger over R index finger and reverse.

My mother has a new baby.

MY
Tap chest with R hand.

MOTHER
R "5," fingertips up, tap chin
with thumb twice.

HAS
Place fingertips of
both hands against
the chest.

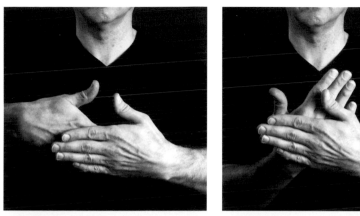

NEW

Open L hand, tips up, palm in. R hand brushes across heel of L from R to L.

BABY

Cradle arms at waist level and rock back and forth.

The man helps the children.

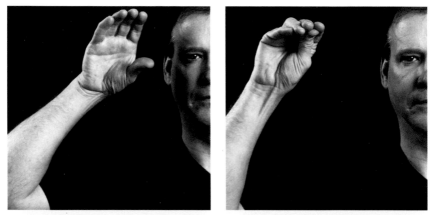

MAN
Mime grabbing brim of a hat with R forefingers and thumb.

HELPS
Place L palm under R "S." Lift hands together.

CHILDREN
Lower R hand, palm down, as if indicating a small child, then bounce to the right.

Those people are deaf.

PEOPLE

R and L "P," palms out, move alternately up and down in a circular motion.

THOSE

Point R index finger toward subjects and move to the R.

ARE

Place tip of R "R" against chin and move forward.

DEAF

Touch R side of mouth with R index finger and move to R ear.

It's cold today.

About the Body

COLD
R and L "S," draw hands close to the body and shiver.

TODAY
Bend both palms up and lower slightly in front of body.

Point R index finger up, point L palm to R elbow, and pivot R arm down to L elbow.

Put on your jacket and hat.

PUT

R and L hands, fingers bunched, move from left to right, opening fingers at end.

ON

Place R palm on back of L hand.

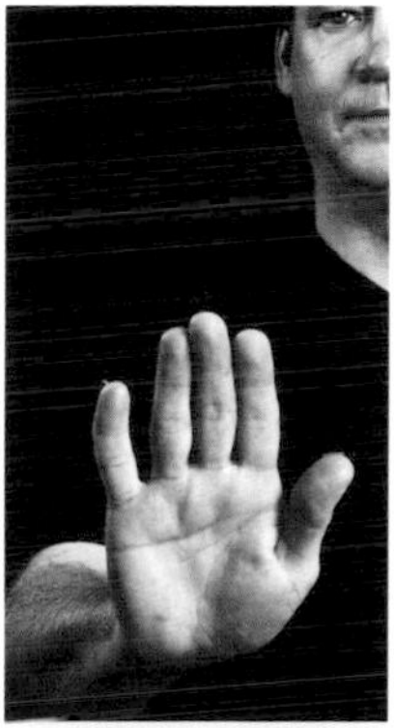

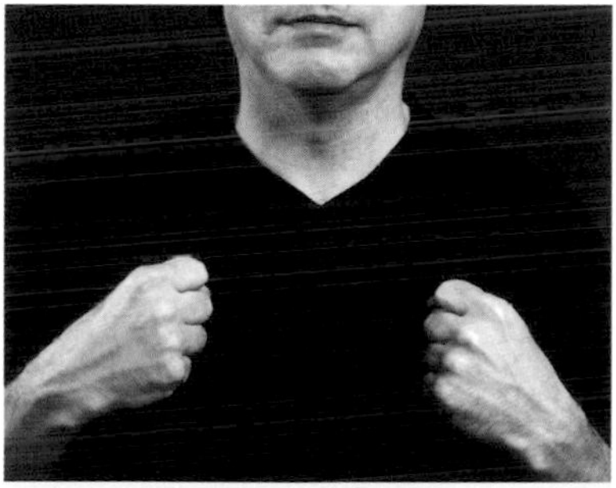

YOUR

Point R palm forward.

JACKET

"A" sign both hands, palms out. Move hands in, as if pulling jacket to body.

HAT

Pat top of head.

That scratch is bleeding.

THAT
Place R "Y" in L palm.

SCRATCH
Outline scratch on palm of L hand with R thumb.

IS
Place little finger of R hand against chin and move it forward.

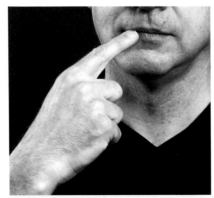

BLEEDING
Touch lips with R index finger.

Move wiggling R fingertips down the back of L hand.

Put a bandage on it.

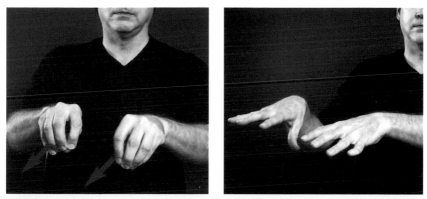

PUT
R and L hands, fingers bunched, move from left to right, opening fingers at end.

BANDAGE
Rub R "H" across back of L palm.

ON
Place R palm on back of L hand.

IT
Place R little finger on palm of L hand.

I am taking a shirt, shoes, and shorts on my vacation.

I'M
"I" hand placed against chest. R "M" moves forward from chin.

TAKE
Draw R hand from R to L, ending in an "S."

SHIRT
Pinch clothing at shoulder to indicate a shirt.

SHOES
"S" sign both hands, palms down, knuckles out, strike together twice.

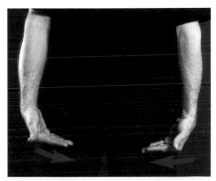

SHORTS

Both hands palms up, fingertips on inside of thighs, move across, outlining bottom of shorts.

ON

Place R palm on back of L hand.

MY

R palm flat on chest.

VACATION

Place thumbs of both hands at armpits and tap twice.

Do you have a stomachache and a fever?

YOU
Point R index finger at subject.

HAVE
Place fingertips of both hands against chest.

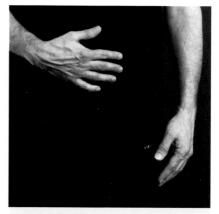

STOMACH
Pat stomach with R hand.

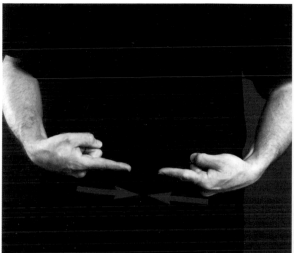

ACHE
Jab index fingers together several times in area.

FEVER
R hand palm out, tips L, place back of hand on forehead.

?
Form question mark in the air with R index finger.

Where are your coat and gloves?

WHERE
Shake R "D" back and forth.

ARE
R "R" at chin, move forward.

YOUR
Point R palm
at subject.

COAT

"A" sign both hands, palms out. Move hands in, as if pulling coat to body.

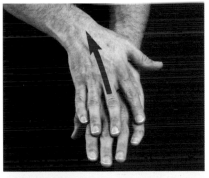

GLOVES

Put R hand over back of L hand, tips out, fingers interlocking, then draw R hand back.

?

Form question mark in the air with R index finger.

Look in your purse for your glasses.

LOOK
Point at eyes with R "V."

Twist and point forward at object.

IN
Place R fingertips
into L "C."

YOUR
Point R palm
at subject.

PURSE
Mime holding purse.

FOR
Touch forehead with R index finger, then turn out and forward.

YOUR
Point R palm at subject.

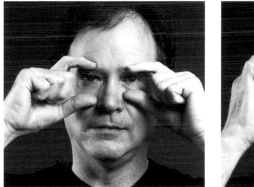

GLASSES
Place thumb and index fingers of both hands on side of eyes. Move away, closing fingers as if outlining frame of glasses.

He needs an emergency operation.

HE
Mime grabbing brim of hat with R forefingers.

Point R index finger at subject.

NEEDS
R "X," pointing down, moves up and down repetitively.

EMERGENCY
R "E," palm out, shake from side to side.

OPERATION
Draw R thumb down side of body.

Please take off your clothes.

PLEASE
Rub open hand in a circle against chest.

TAKE
Draw R hand from R to L, ending in an "S."

OFF
Place R palm on back of L hand and lift off.

YOUR
Point R palm at subject.

CLOTHES
Both hands palms in, brush down chest twice.

63

The blind man was sick in the hospital.

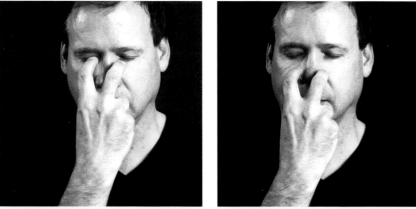

BLIND
Touch eyes with R "V" and draw down the face slightly.

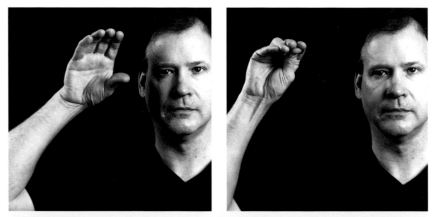

MAN
Mime grabbing brim of hat.

WAS
Move R "W" back, ending in an "S."

SICK
Tap forehead with
R middle finger and
stomach with L
middle finger.

IN
Place R fingertips
into L "C."

HOSPITAL
Make cross on
L upper arm with
R "H."

Drink this water with your pill.

DRINK
Bring R "C" to mouth as if holding a glass.

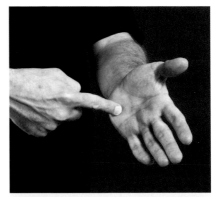

THIS
Place tip of R index finger in upturned L palm.

WATER
Tap chin twice with index finger of R "W."

WITH
Place R and L "A" together, palm to palm.

YOUR
Point R palm at subject.

PILL
Mime taking a pill with thumb and index finger.

He broke his arm in the accident.

HE
Mime grabbing brim of hat.

Point R index finger at subject.

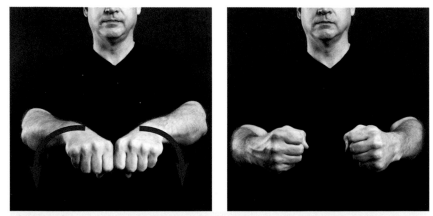

BROKE
Hold R and L "S" palm down, side by side, and twist down.

HIS
Move palm out toward subject.

ARM
Pass R fingertips down L arm.

IN
Place R fingertips into L "C."

ACCIDENT
R and L "S," knuckles facing, strike together.

When I wake up I brush my teeth.

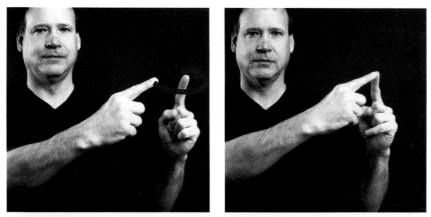

WHEN
Draw a circle in the air with R index finger and tap L index finger.

I
"I" hand placed against chest.

WAKE UP
Place R and L "Q" at sides of closed eyes, forefingers and thumbs touching. Separate and open eyes.

I
"I" hand placed against chest.

BRUSH MY TEETH
Rub R index finger back and forth across teeth.

Every morning she cooks her breakfast.

EVERY
Hold up L "A" and use inside of thumb of R "A" to stroke back of L thumb.

MORNING
Place fingertips of R hand in crook of L arm. Raise L arm to vertical position.

SHE
Draw R thumb down side of cheek.

Point at subject.

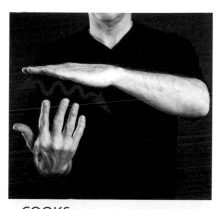

COOKS
L hand palm down, R underneath.
Wiggle R fingers.

HER
Move palm out toward subject.

BREAKFAST
Tap bunched hand at mouth
several times.

Place fingertips of R hand in
crook of L arm. Raise L arm to
vertical position.

They listen to the news on the radio.

THEY
Point R index finger
toward subjects
and move to R.

LISTEN
Place tip of R index
finger at ear.

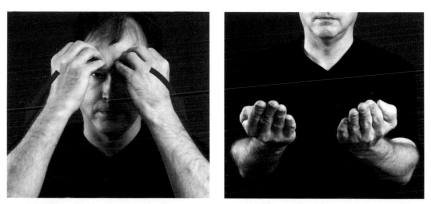

NEWS

Place bunched hands at forehead. Move down and away, ending with palms up.

ON

Place R palm on back of L hand.

RADIO

Place cupped hands over ears.

Please open the door.

PLEASE
Rub open hand in a circle against chest.

OPEN
R and L "B," palms down, tips out, index fingers touching. Pull apart, ending with palms up and facing each other.

DOOR
"B" sign both hands, palms out, tips slightly raised, with index fingers touching. Turn R hand to R, ending with palm L, then return to starting position.

Pour me a drink.

POUR
"A" sign R hand, arc to L, pointing thumb toward ground.

ME
Tap index finger to chest.

DRINK
Bring R "C" to mouth as if holding a glass.

My body is cold.

MY

R palm on chest.

BODY

Both hands palms in, tips facing. Pat upper chest, then stomach.

IS

Place little finger of R hand against chin and move it forward.

COLD

"S" sign both hands, knuckles facing. Bring hands close to body and pretend to shiver.

I wear warm clothes.

I
R "I" placed against chest.

WEAR
Both hands palms in, brush down chest twice.

WARM
Place tips of R "A" at chin, then open into a "5."

CLOTHES
Both hands palms in, brush down chest twice.

Her son is deaf and wears a hearing aid.

HER
Move palm out toward subject.

SON
Mime grabbing brim of hat.

Place R hand, palm up, in crook of L arm.

IS
Place little finger of R hand against chin and move it forward.

DEAF
R index finger at chin, then move to ear.

WEARS
Both hands palms in, brush down chest twice.

HEARING AID
R index and middle fingers are placed on the ear, as if inserting a hearing aid.

My foot is bleeding.

MY
Tap chest with R palm.

FOOT
L hand palm down, move thumb and index finger of R "F" around edge of L fingertips.

IS
Place little finger of R hand against chin and move it forward.

BLEEDING
R index finger at mouth. Trickle R fingers down back of L hand to indicate dripping blood.

Did you cut your leg?

YOU
Point R index finger
at subject.

CUT
Move R thumb
across L palm.

YOUR
Point R palm at
subject.

LEG
Pat R thigh with R hand.

?
Form question mark in the air
with R index finger.

Does the medicine taste bad?

MEDICINE
Circle R middle
finger on L palm.

TASTE
R "5," palm in.
Tap middle finger
on tongue.

BAD
Touch lips with fingers of R hand, then turn palm down.

?
Form question mark in the air with R index finger.

Do you talk in your sleep?

YOU
Point R index finger at subject.

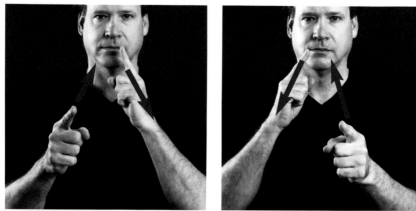

TALK
Place index fingers on mouth, alternately moving back and forth.

IN
Place R fingertips into L "C."

YOUR
Point R palm at subject.

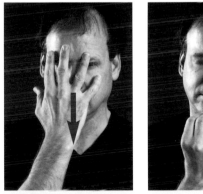

SLEEP
R "5," palm in, fingers over eyes. Slide down face, ending in an "O."

?
Form question mark in the air with R index finger.

What is the temperature on your thermometer?

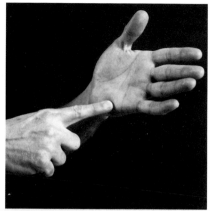

WHAT
Draw tip of R index finger down L palm.

IS
Place little finger of R hand against chin and move it forward.

TEMPERATURE
L and R "1," L palm out, R palm down. Rub R index finger up and down between first and second joints of L index finger.

ON
Place R palm on back of L hand.

YOUR
Point R palm at subject.

THERMOMETER
L and R "1," L palm out, R palm down. Rub R index finger up and down between first and second joints of L index finger.

?
Form question mark in the air with R index finger.

It's raining. Stand under the umbrella.

RAINING

Tap chin several times with index finger of R "W." Lower R and L "5" twice, palms down.

STAND

L palm up, tips out. Stand tips of R "V" on L palm.

UNDER

Move R "A" under L hand, palm down.

UMBRELLA

Put R "S" on top of L "S" and pull apart, as if opening an umbrella.

Her father wears pajamas and a robe.

HER
Move palm out toward subject.

FATHER
Tap the forehead twice with thumb of R "5."

WEARS
Both hands palms in, brush down chest twice.

PAJAMAS
Finger spell "P" and "J."

ROBE
R and L "R," palms
in, tips facing.
Brush down chest.

I need shampoo and soap for the shower.

School and Home

NEED
R "X," pointing down, move up and down several times.

I
"I" hand placed against chest.

SHAMPOO
Place tips of both hands on head and rub back and forth, as if shampooing hair.

SOAP
L hand palm up, tips out, R palm tips down. Draw R fingers backward across L palm.

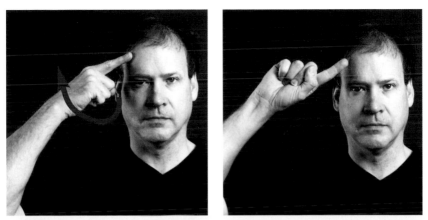

FOR
Touch forehead with R index finger, then turn out and forward.

SHOWER
R "S" held above the head, open into a "5" sign and repeat.

Would you like a toothbrush, toothpaste, and a towel?

WOULD
Place R "W" near face and draw forward into a "D."

YOU
Point R index finger
at subject.

LIKE
Place thumb and middle finger against chest
and move them away from body, touching tips.

TOOTHBRUSH
Rub R index finger across mouth.

TOOTHPASTE
Mime spreading toothpaste on toothbrush with R "P."

TOWEL
Both hands palms in, tips up.
Circle fingertips on cheeks.

?
Form question mark in the air with R index finger.

There is a radio and television in your room.

THERE
Point at object.

IS
Place little finger of R hand against chin and move it forward.

RADIO
Place cupped hands over ears.

TELEVISION
Finger spell "T" and "V."

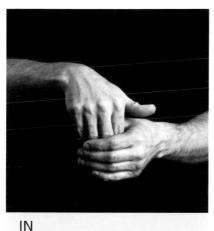

IN
Place R fingertips into L "C."

YOUR
Point R palm at subject.

ROOM
Mime making a square. Place open hands in front of body, with palms facing body, and move hands to make palms face each other.

Your bed has blue sheets and green blankets.

YOUR
Point R palm at subject.

BED
Tilt head slightly to R, with R palm on R cheek.

HAS
Tips of both hands on chest.

BLUE
R "B," shake back and forth.

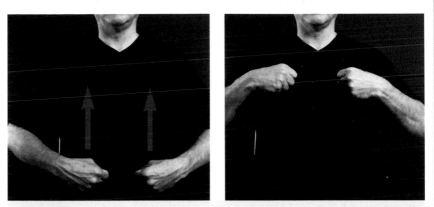

SHEETS

Both hands "S," knuckles down. Move up from waist to chest as if pulling up a sheet.

GREEN

R "G," shake back and forth.

BLANKETS

Both hands "B," palms down, fingertips facing. Move up from waist to chest.

The curtains are orange and brown.

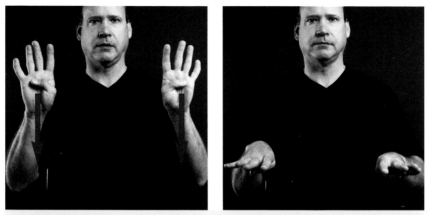

CURTAINS
Both hands "4," drop forward and down, ending with palms down.

ARE
"R" at chin, move forward.

ORANGE
Open and close R "S" at chin two times.

BROWN
Place R "B" on R cheek and slide down.

The telephone is on the table under the window.

TELEPHONE
R "Y," place thumb on ear and little finger on mouth.

IS
Place little finger of R hand against chin and move it forward.

ON
Place R palm on back of L hand.

TABLE
Place R forearm on L forearm.

UNDER
Move R "A" under downturned L palm.

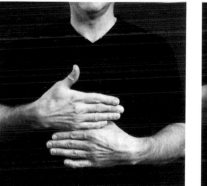 

WINDOW
Palms of both hands facing chest, tips opposite. Place R little finger on top of L index finger, touching. Move R hand up and down.

The paper, pencil, scissors, and crayons are in the basket.

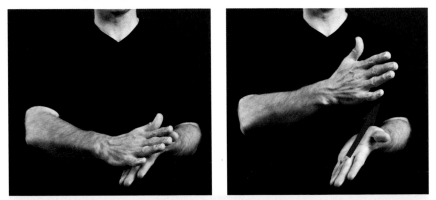

PAPER

L hand palm up, tips out. R hand palm down, tips L. Brush R palm across L palm twice, toward the body.

PENCIL

L hand palm up, tips R. Touch tips of R thumb and index finger to mouth, then slide across L palm as if writing.

SCISSORS
Palm in, alternate
"U" and "V."

CRAYONS
Move R "C" across
L palm with wavy
motion.

ARE
R "R" at chin, move
forward.

IN
Place R fingertips
into L "C."

BASKET
Place R index finger under L wrist and swing to
L elbow.

There is tape, string, and a camera in the desk drawer.

THERE
Point at object.

IS
Place little finger of R hand against chin and move it forward.

TAPE
R and L "H," palms down, fingertips touching. Move apart in a straight line.

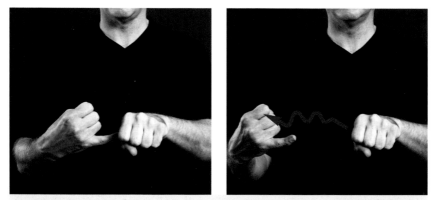

STRING
L "S," palm down. Place tip of R small finger on L "S" and shake away to R in wavy motion.

CAMERA
Mime taking a photograph.

IN
Place R fingertips into L "C."

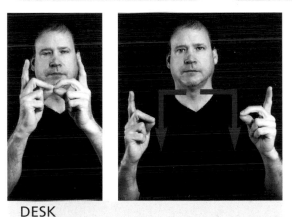

DESK
"D" sign both hands, palms facing, draw apart and down.

DRAWER
Cupped R and L hands extended, pull toward body.

The letter came in today's mail.

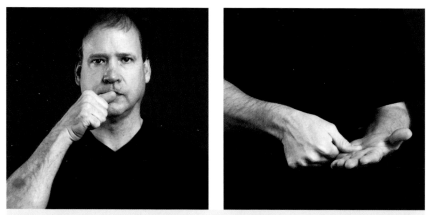

LETTER
Place thumb of R "A" on mouth and then on upturned L palm.

CAME
Index fingers rotating around each other move toward the body.

IN
Place R fingertips into L "C."

TODAY'S

Palms up, lower slightly in front of body.

Point R index finger up, point L arm at R elbow, and pivot R arm down to L elbow.

MAIL

Place thumb of R "A" on mouth and then on upturned L palm.

ATTENTION

Palms facing in front of face, move forward quickly in parallel to one another, then repeat.

FIRE

R and L "5," palms in, move up while wiggling fingers.

ALARM

L hand, tips up and palm R, strike with R "X," knuckles down. Repeat.

The blanket is purple and the pillow is white.

PURPLE
R "P," shake back and forth from wrist.

BLANKET
R and L "B," palms in, fingertips facing. Move up chest.

PILLOW
Place back of L hand on right cheek, tilt head to R, mime patting underside of pillow with R hand.

WHITE
R "5," palm in, tips L. Place R fingertips on chest and draw out into "O."

There is a large mirror in the bathroom.

THERE
Point at object.

IS
Place little finger of R hand against chin and move it forward.

LARGE
R and L "L," facing each other with index fingers bent, are drawn apart.

MIRROR

R hand, palm in front of face, twist slightly to R and repeat.

IN
Place R fingertips into L "C."

BATHROOM (TOILET)
R "T," shake back and forth.

It is on the shelf in the kitchen.

IT
Tap L palm with R little finger.

IS
Place little finger of R hand against chin and move it forward.

ON
Place R palm on back of L hand.

SHELF
Both hands palms down, tips out, held at shoulder level. Hold together and move apart in straight line.

IN
Place R fingertips into L "C."

KITCHEN
Place palm of R "K" on L palm and reverse "K."

A curtain hangs in front of the door.

CURTAIN
R and L "4," hold up at shoulder height, then drop forward and down, ending with palms down.

HANGS
Place R "X" on L index finger.

IN
Place R fingertips into L "C."

FRONT

Place R hand, palm in and tips to L, in front of forehead and drop in front of face.

DOOR

"B" sign both hands, palms out, tips slightly raised with index fingers together. Then turn R hand to R, ending with palm L, and return to starting position.

Put the lamp on the piano, please.

PUT
R and L hands, fingers bunched, move from L to R, opening fingers at end.

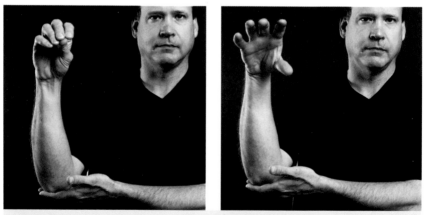

LAMP
R "O," palm down, open R fingers into a "5," palm down.

ON
Place R palm on back of L hand.

PIANO
Mime playing a piano.

PLEASE
Rub R palm in circle on chest.

The noise came from the class meeting.

NOISE
R and L "5" held at ears, palms down. Shake outward.

CAME
Index fingers rotating around each other move toward the body.

FROM
L index finger pointing R, palm in. R "X," palm in, knuckles of R index finger against L index finger. Pull R hand toward body.

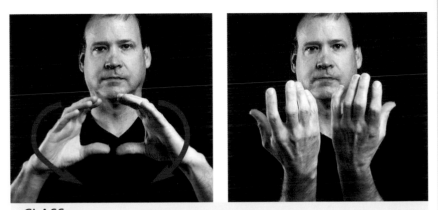

CLASS

R and L "C" facing each other. Draw around in an arc to the front and forward, complete arc with little fingers touching and palms in.

MEETING

R and L "D," palms facing, tips up. Bring together, hands touching.

Leisure

MERRY
Both hands palms in, tips facing. Brush up the chest twice.

CHRISTMAS
Arc R "C" from L to R at shoulder height.

Pray to God.

PRAY
Place palms together, tips out. Rotate toward body, ending with tips up.

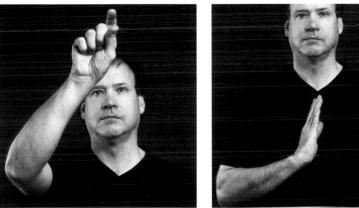

GOD
R "G" above head, move down to chest, ending in a "B" on chest.

Santa's reindeer pull his sleigh.

SANTA
R "C" at chin, bring down to chest.

REINDEER
Thumbs of R and L "5" at the sides of the head; draw away.

PULL
Mime pulling a rope.

HIS
Move R palm out.

SLEIGH
"X" sign both hands, palms in. Arc outward, ending with palm up, and draw back toward body.

We decorate the church for Easter Sunday.

WE

Place R index finger on R shoulder and circle around until it touches L shoulder.

DECORATE

R and L "O," L palm up, R palm down. Touch tips and reverse positions several times while moving from L to R.

CHURCH
Tap R "C" on back of L hand twice.

FOR
R index finger at forehead, turn finger out.

EASTER
Arc R "E" from l to R in front of body.

SUNDAY
R and L palms out in front of body, move down slightly as if patting.

Did you receive a valentine card?

YOU
Point R index finger at subject.

RECEIVE
R and L "5" in front of body, move in toward body and finish in "S," placing one hand above the other.

VALENTINE
Make shape of heart on L chest with tips of R and L "V."

CARD
Palms together, then open.

?
Form question mark in the air with R index finger.

She wraps the present with colored paper.

SHE

Put thumb of R "A" on cheek and draw a line along jaw, then point at subject.

WRAP

Both hands palms in, L tips R, R tips L; circle L hand around R.

WITH

Bring R and L "A" together.

PRESENT

"P" shape both hands, bring up and turn out.

COLORED

R "5," palm in, wiggle fingers at chin level.

PAPER

L hand palm up, tips out. R hand palm down, tips L. Brush R palm across L palm twice.

133

It was a magic puzzle.

IT

Tap L palm with R
little finger.

WAS

Move R "W" sign back, ending in an "S."

PUZZLE

R and L "A" sign,
palms down. Place
together as if trying
to make them fit.

MAGIC

R and L "O," palms down, move away from
the body in a semicircle, opening into a "5."

The party was a surprise.

PARTY

R and L "P," palms down. Swing hands to L and R several times.

WAS

Move R "W" sign back, ending in an "S."

SURPRISE

Place both index fingers and thumbs at side of head. Snap both hands open into "L."

Do you play tennis, baseball, or football?

YOU

Point R index finger at subject.

PLAY

Place R and L "Y" in front of body and shake back and forth several times.

TENNIS

Mime swinging a tennis racket.

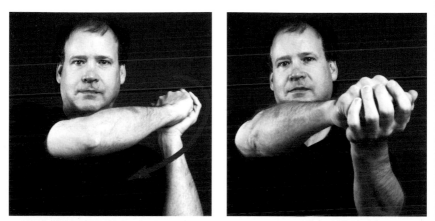

BASEBALL
Mime grasping a bat and swinging it.

FOOTBALL
"5" sign both hands, palms in, tips facing. Link fingers together several times.

?
Form question mark in the air with R index finger.

He had a toy drum for his birthday.

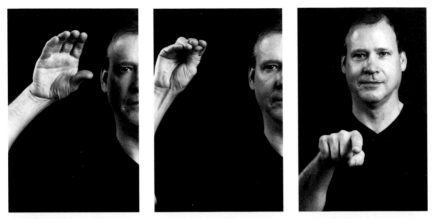

HE
Mime grabbing the brim of a hat, then point R index finger at subject.

HAD
Tips of both hands against chest.

TOY
R and L "T," swing in and out twice.

DRUM
Mime holding drumsticks and beating a drum.

FOR
Point R index finger at forehead and turn finger out.

HIS
Push palm out toward subject.

BIRTHDAY
Back of R hand over L palm, push out.

R index finger up, L hand at R elbow, R hand to L elbow.

Follow your dream.

Actions

FOLLOW
"A" sign both hands, thumbs up, R behind L, move forward together.

YOUR
Point R palm at subject.

DREAM
Place R index finger on forehead, move away from head, bending finger several times.

Learn to write.

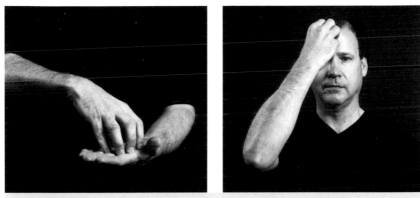

LEARN

L palm up, tips out. Place fingertips of R "C" on L palm, then move to the forehead, changing into an "O" with tips on forehead.

WRITE

L palm up, tips out. Mime writing on L palm with closed R index finger and thumb.

I want to wish you a good visit.

I
R "I" placed against chest.

WANT
Cupped "5" hands in front of body, pull toward chest.

WISH
"C" sign at chest, palm in, draw down.

YOU
Point R index finger at subject.

GOOD
Touch lips with fingers of R hand, then forward into palm of L hand.

VISIT
R and L "V" in front of body, tips up, draw toward body in circular motion.

She helped the woman button her dress.

SHE
Put thumb of R "A" on cheek and draw a line along jaw, then point.

HELP
Place R "S" on upturned L palm and raise hands together.

WOMAN
R "A" on cheek, draw line along jaw, finish with "5" on chest.

BUTTON
R "F," palm down. Tap chest
three times, moving downward.

HER
Palm out toward subject.

DRESS
Brush down chest with fingertips several times.

The blind man could feel the wall.

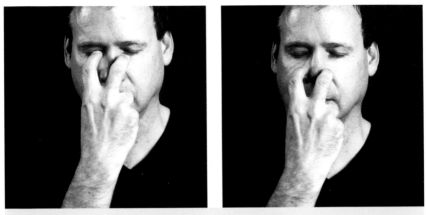

BLIND
Touch eyes with R "V" and move fingers down nose.

MAN
Mime grabbing the brim of a hat.

COULD
Lower R and L "S," palms down.

FEEL
Place tip of R middle finger against chest, with other fingers extended. Draw up.

WALL
R and L "W" held together, palms in. Move apart.

Hurry. Go out and play.

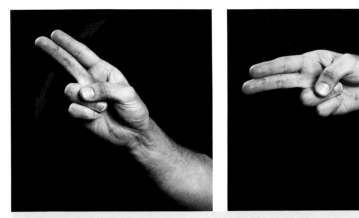

HURRY

"H" sign both hands, palms facing, tips out. Shake up and down.

GO

R and L "1," palms in. Rotate hands out several times.

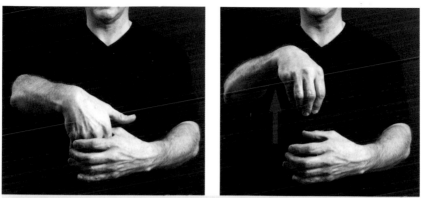

OUT

R fingers drawn out of L "C," both palms in, bunch up fingertips of R hand as it comes out.

PLAY

"Y" sign both hands, palms in, twist back and forth.

Find the belt for your skirt.

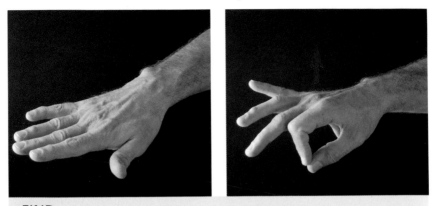

FIND

R "5" sign, palm down, tips out. Close thumb and index finger into "F" and raise hand as if pulling something up.

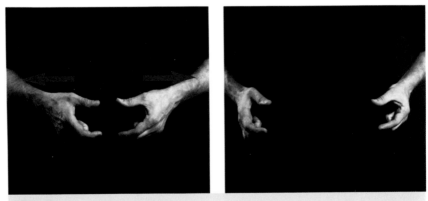

BELT

Move R and L "L," palms facing and index fingers bent, from middle of stomach to sides.

FOR
Touch forehead with R index finger, then turn out and push forward.

YOUR
Point R palm at subject.

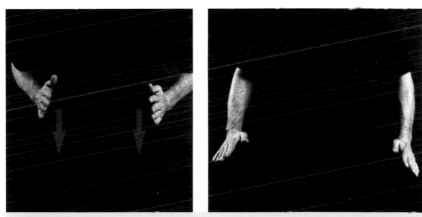

SKIRT
Both hands palms down, thumbs on waist. Brush down.

Remember to pay for your laundry.

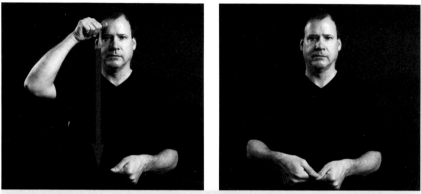

REMEMBER

Place thumb of R "A" on forehead, then drop down and touch thumb of L "A."

PAY

L hand palm up, tips out. Place index finger of R hand on L palm and flick out.

FOR
Touch forehead with R index finger, then turn out and push forward.

YOUR
Point R palm at subject.

LAUNDRY
Knuckles of R and L "A" touching, rub together.

Don't worry, the toothpaste will help keep your teeth white.

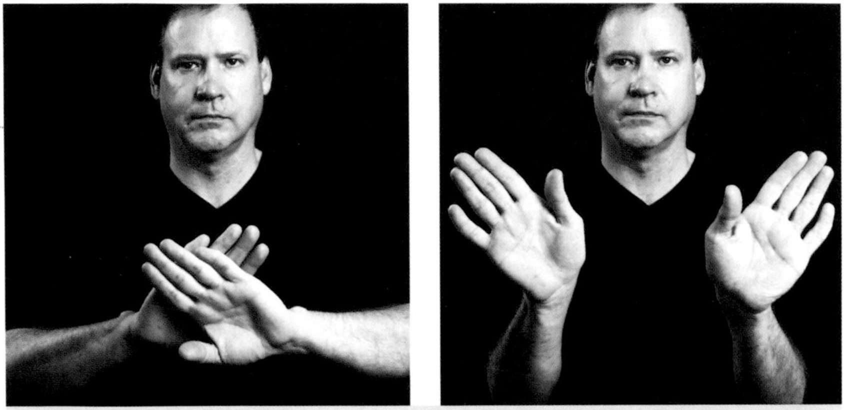

NOT

Cross "5" hands, palms facing out and separate. Repeat movement.

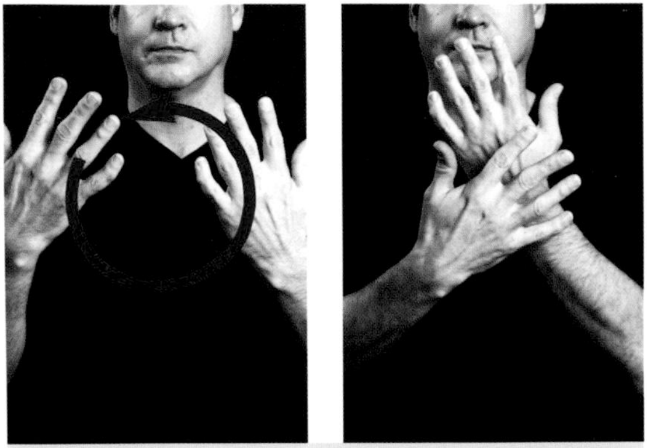

WORRY

R and L palms in, circle alternately in front of head.

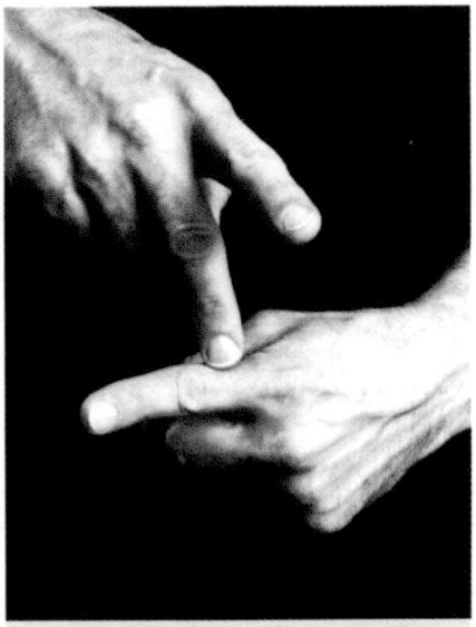

TOOTHPASTE

Middle finger of R "P," move along L index finger.

WILL
R hand at cheek, palm L, move forward.

HELP
R "S," palm L, place in L palm and raise L palm up.

KEEP
"V" sign both hands, tips out. Place R "V" on L "V."

YOUR
Point R palm at subject.

TEETH
Outline teeth with R index finger.

WHITE
R "5," palm in, tips on chest. Draw away from chest into an "O."

155

Please try to continue working.

PLEASE
Rub R palm in circle on chest.

TRY
R and L "T," palms in. Move forward and arc down.

CONTINUE
Place R thumb on top of L thumb and push down.

WORK
R "S," palm down, tap twice on wrist of L "S."

Where do you live?

WHERE
Shake R index finger back and forth, palm out.

YOU
Point R index finger at subject.

LIVE
R and L "L," palms to body. Brush up chest.

?
Form question mark in the air with R index finger.

My uncle broke his arm in an accident.

MY
R palm flat on chest.

UNCLE
R "U," wiggle at R temple.

BROKE
"S" sign both hands, palms down, thumbs and index fingers touching, then separate.

HIS
Palm out toward subject.

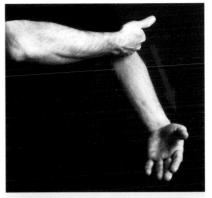

ARM
Touch L wrist with R hand and move along arm to elbow.

IN
Place R fingertips into L "C."

ACCIDENT
R and L "A," palms in and knuckles facing, strike together.

Those people are waiting to take a test.

THOSE
Point at subjects and move in arc to the R.

PEOPLE
R and L "P," palms out, move alternately up and down in circular motion.

ARE
"R" sign at chin, move forward.

WAITING

Both hands palms up, tips out, in front of body, and slightly to L. Wiggle fingers.

TAKE

R "5," palm down. Draw up quickly, ending in an "S."

TEST

Draw question marks with both hands, then open hands.

I forgot my robe and slippers.

I
Place R "I" against chest.

FORGOT
R hand palm in, tips L. Draw across forehead from L to R, ending in an "A."

MY
R palm flat on chest.

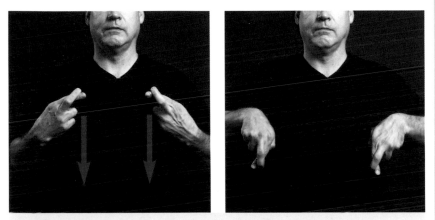

ROBE

"R" sign both hands, palms in, tips facing. Brush down chest.

SLIPPERS

L "C," palm down. R hand palm down, tips L. Slide R hand through L "C" and repeat.

Flowers are growing in the garden.

Nature

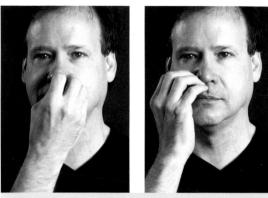

FLOWERS
R "O," place tips on R side of nose, then arc to L side of nose.

ARE
"R" sign at chin, move forward.

GROW
L "C" in front of body, palm in. Pass R "O" up and through L "C," spreading fingers as hand emerges.

IN
Place R fingertips into L "C."

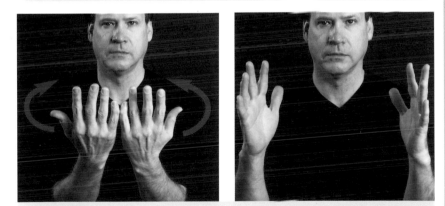

GARDEN
R and L "5" in front of body, palms in. Move away from each other to the sides, then toward the body.

My dog hates grooming.

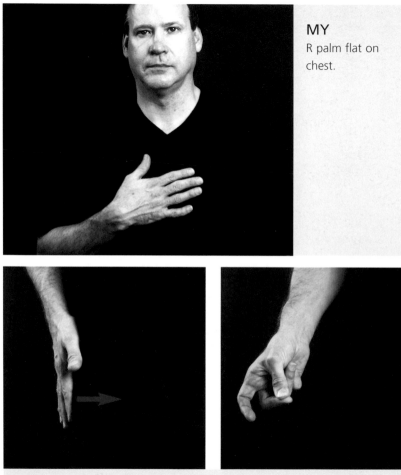

MY
R palm flat on chest.

DOG
Slap R thigh with R hand, then snap R thumb and middle finger.

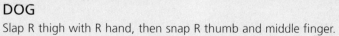

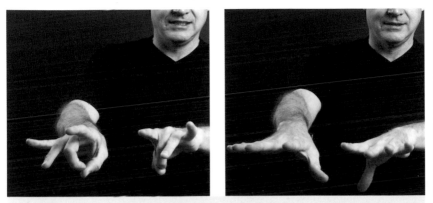

HATE

R and L palms down, thumb and middle fingers touching. Push away from body, snapping middle fingers to form "5" with both hands.

GROOMING

Alternate R "V" and "U," palm up. Move up L arm, miming a snipping action.

There is a rainbow in the sky.

THERE
Point at object.

IS
Place little finger of R hand against chin and move it forward.

RAINBOW
Hold R hand near mouth and wiggle fingers.

R "B," palm down, placed above head, move from L to R. End with fingertips pointing up.

IN
Place R fingertips
into L "C."

SKY
R "B," palm down,
placed above head,
move from L to R.
End with fingertips
pointing up.

On the farm we have cows and chickens.

FARM
R "5," palm L. Place thumb on L side of chin and draw across to R side of chin.

ON
Place R palm on back of L hand.

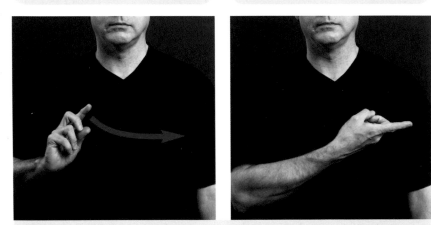

WE
Place R index finger at R shoulder and circle around to L shoulder.

HAVE
Place fingertips of both hands at chest.

COWS
Place thumb of R "Y" on R temple, palm out, then twist down.

CHICKENS
Place thumb and index finger of R "G" on mouth, then place fingertips on L palm.

It was a cat and mouse story.

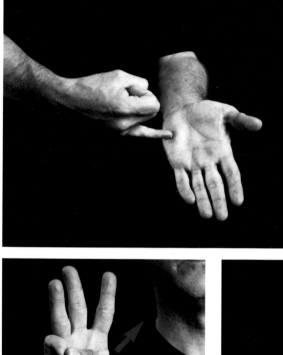

IT
Place R little finger
on palm of L hand.

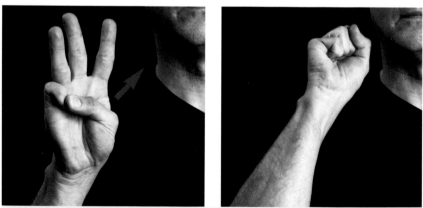

WAS
Move R "W" back, ending in an "S."

CAT
Place R and L "F" on mouth, palms out, and pull away twice.

MOUSE
Strike tip of nose twice with R index finger.

STORY
Join "F" sign of both hands like links in a chain, then separate twice.

The lions are behind a fence at the zoo.

LIONS
R "5," tips down. Place above head and move to back of neck.

ARE
"R" sign from chin, move forward.

BEHIND
Place R and L "A" together, palms facing. Move R behind L.

FENCE

"5" sign both hands, palm in, tips facing. Place tips of middle fingers together, then draw apart.

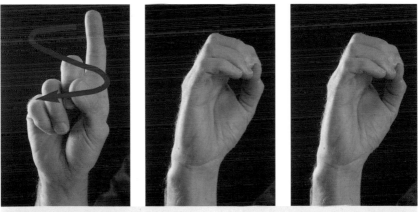

ZOO

Finger spell "zoo."

The monkey sat in the tree.

MONKEY
Scratch the sides of the body with both hands.

SAT
Place curved R index and middle fingers over L "H" sign, palms down.

IN
Place R fingertips into L "C."

TREE
R "5" sign, palm L. Place R elbow on back of L hand and shake R hand back and forth.

There are turtles in the water.

THERE
Point at object.

ARE
"R" sign from chin, move forward.

TURTLES
Place R "A" under curved L hand. Extend thumb and wiggle.

IN
Place R fingertips into L "C."

WATER
Tap chin twice with index finger of R "W."

The moon and stars light the way through the woods.

STARS
"1" sign both hands, palms out. Repeatedly strike index fingers upward against each other.

MOON
Place R "C" at side of R eye.

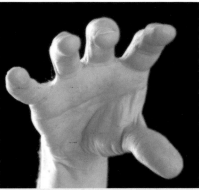

LIGHT
R hand fingertips together palm down. Open fingers into "5" sign, palm down.

WAY
"W" sign both hands, palms facing, tips out. Move forward.

THROUGH
With L hand facing body, move R hand between index and middle finger of L hand.

WOODS
R "W," palm L. Place R elbow on back of L hand and twist R hand back and forth.

The pig is dirty.

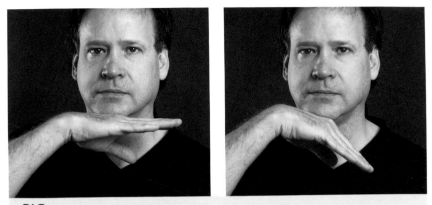

PIG
Place back of R hand, fingers together, under chin and flap up and down twice.

IS
Place little finger of R hand against chin and move it forward.

DIRTY
R hand placed under chin, palm down. Wiggle fingers.

The pony ran across the road.

PONY
R "P," place thumb knuckle on R temple, twist down twice.

RAN
Hook curved index finger of R "L" around the thumb of the L "L" and move forward.

ACROSS
L hand palm down, tips R, pass R hand across back of the L hand.

ROAD
"R" sign both hands, palms in, tips out. Move forward.

She rides her horse on the beach.

SHE
Put thumb of R "A" on cheek and draw a line along jaw, then point.

RIDES
Place curved R "U" in L "O" and move forward.

HER
Move palm out at subject.

HORSE
Place R "H" on R temple and flap "H" sign up and down twice.

ON
Place R palm on back of L hand.

BEACH
"B" sign both hands, palms down, L tips slanted R, R tips slanted L. Circle R hand over L arm to elbow, then back.

They had sun, rain, snow, and wind in a day.

THEY
Point R index finger at subjects and move in arc to R.

HAD
Tips of both hands against chest.

SUN
Draw a circle with R index finger.

RAIN
"5" sign both hands, palms down, tips out. Move quickly down two or three times.

SNOW

Hold fingertips against chest and draw forward into an "O."

Lower "5" hands down while wiggling fingers.

WIND

R and L "5," palms facing, tips out. Swing back and forth.

IN

Place R fingertips into L "C."

DAY

Point R index finger up, back of L hand under R elbow, pivot R hand down to L elbow.

There are birds on the grass in the yard.

THERE
Point at object.

ARE
"R" sign from chin, move forward.

BIRDS
"G" sign R hand. Place on mouth and snap index finger and thumb together twice.

ON
Place R palm on back of L hand.

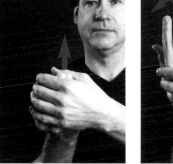
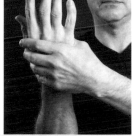

GRASS

Wiggle R "G."

L "C" in front of body, palm in. Pass R "O" sign through L "C," spreading fingers as hand emerges. Move R hand to R, wiggling fingers.

YARD

L "B," palm down. R "Y," palm down. Circle R "Y" over L hand and forearm.

IN

Place R fingertips into L "C."

The rabbit ran across the street and into the barn.

RABBIT
"H" sign both hands, cross at the wrist and wiggle "H" fingers up and down.

RAN
Hook curved index finger of R "L" around the thumb of the L "L" and move forward.

ACROSS
With L hand palm down, tips R, pass R hand across back of the L hand.

STREET
"S" sign both hands, palms facing. Move forward.

INTO
Place R fingertips into L "C."

BARN
"B" sign both hands, palms out and index fingers touching. Draw hands apart and then down.

My boots are wet.

Descriptions

MY
R palm on chest.

BOOTS
R "C," palm down.
Slide L "B," palm
down, under R "C"
and repeat.

ARE
"R" sign from chin,
move forward.

WET
L "5" in front of body, palm in. Index finger of
R "W" on chin. Drop both into "O" signs.

She was thirsty.

SHE
Put thumb of R "A" on cheek and draw a line along jaw, then point.

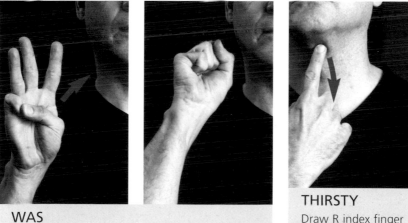

WAS
Move R "W" sign back, ending in an "S."

THIRSTY
Draw R index finger down throat.

Watch the beautiful butterfly.

WATCH

Put R "V" in front of face, then turn "V" away from body.

BEAUTIFUL

"5" sign R hand, palm in, tips up. Circle face from R to L, ending in an "O" sign at chin, then open fingers, palm in, tips up.

BUTTERFLY

Palms in, hook thumbs together. Flap fingers.

It was a hot and lazy afternoon.

IT
Place R small finger on palm of L hand.

WAS
Move R "W" sign back, ending in an "S."

HOT
Place R "5" sign, fingers bent, in front of chin. Turn out and away from body.

LAZY
R "L" sign, palm in. Tap twice just below L shoulder.

AFTERNOON
L arm in front of body, palm down, pointing R. R forearm, palm down, on back of L hand, pointing slightly upward.

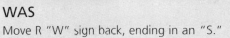

Her hair was long.

HER
Palm out toward subject.

HAIR
Grab strand of hair with R thumb and index finger.

WAS
Move R "W" sign back, ending in an "S."

LONG
L arm extended in front of body. Run R index finger up L arm.

My father is funny when he is angry.

MY
R palm on chest.

FATHER
R "5," tap forehead with thumb twice.

IS
R little finger on chin, move forward.

FUNNY
Brush nose twice with tips of R "H" sign.

WHEN
Draw a circle in the air with R index finger and tap L index finger.

HE

Mime grabbing brim of hat with R forefingers.

Point R index finger at subject.

IS

Place little finger of R hand against chin and move it forward.

ANGRY

R and L "5," palms in, tips bent, move up from chest to shoulders.

The bear is large and heavy.

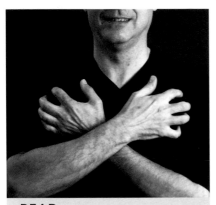

BEAR
Cross wrists of clawed hands and scratch upper chest.

IS
Place little finger of R hand against chin and move it forward.

LARGE
"L" signs, palms facing, thumbs up. Move hands apart.

HEAVY
Both hands palms up, tips out, lower slowly.

That person is nice and quiet.

THAT
Place R "Y" in upturned L palm.

PERSON
Both hands "P" sign, palms down, fingertips out, with wrist against side of body. Move down body.

IS
Place little finger of R hand against chin and move it forward.

NICE
R palm on top of L palm, move from L to R.

QUIET
R index finger at mouth, palm L. Open both hands down and to the side, palms facing.

The duck is happy in the water.

DUCK
Snap thumb, middle finger, and index finger at the mouth twice.

IS
Place little finger of R hand against chin and move it forward.

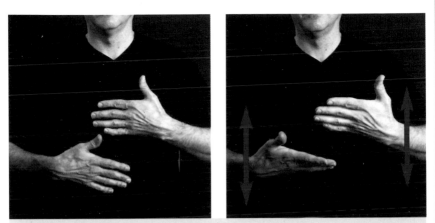

HAPPY
R and L palms in against chest, brush up and down twice.

IN
Place R fingertips into L "C."

WATER
Tap chin twice with index finger of R "W," palm facing L.

The child was afraid to be alone.

CHILD
Lower R hand,
palm down.

WAS
Move R "W" sign back, ending in an "S."

AFRAID
"5" sign both hands, palms in, tips facing.
Move in and out several times as if shaking
with fear.

ALONE
"1" sign R hand,
palm in. Circle
counterclockwise.

They were the same color.

THEY
Point R index finger at subject and move in arc to R.

WERE
Move R "W" sign back, ending in an "R."

SAME
"1" sign both hands, palms down, tips out. Bring index fingers together.

COLOR
R "5" sign, palm in, wiggle fingers at chin level.

It was a small, old book.

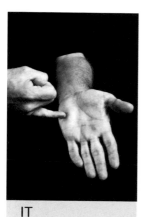

IT
Place R small finger on palm of L hand.

WAS
Move R "W" sign back, ending in an "S."

SMALL
Palms facing, tips out. Draw close together.

OLD

Place R "S" under chin, palm in, and move down in a wavy motion.

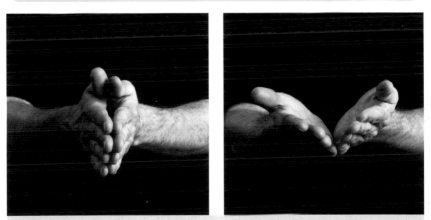

BOOK

Palms together, thumbs up, open as if opening a book.

The refrigerator was clean and new.

REFRIGERATOR
"R" sign both hands, tips out, shake back and forth in shivering motion.

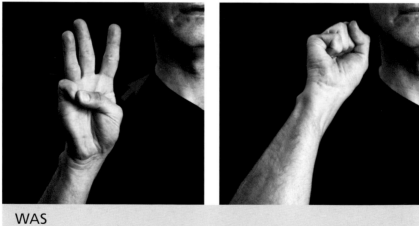

WAS
Move R "W" sign back, ending in an "S."

CLEAN
L palm up, tips R.
R palm down, tips L.
Brush R across L as if
wiping clean.

NEW
L hand palm up, tips out. Brush back of R hand inward across L palm.

It was cold and dry sitting on the floor.

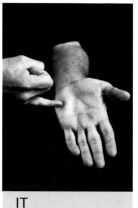

IT
Place R small finger on L palm.

WAS
Move R "W" sign back, ending in an "S."

COLD
"S" sign both hands, knuckles facing. Bring hands close to body and pretend to shiver.

DRY
Move R "X" from L to R across chin.

SIT
Place curved R index and middle fingers crosswise over L "H," palms down.

ON
Place R palm on back of L hand.

FLOOR
Both hands "B" sign, palms down, index fingers touching. Move apart.

Two cups of coffee, please.

Eating and Drinking

TWO
Hold up two fingers.

CUPS
Place R "C" sign on upturned L palm.

COFFEE
Place R "S" on top of L "S" and make a counterclockwise grinding motion.

PLEASE
Rub R palm in circle on chest.

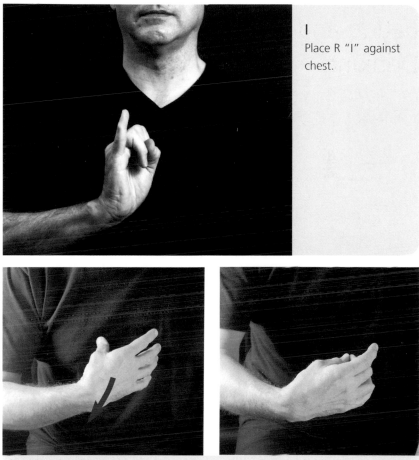

I
Place R "I" against chest.

LIKE
Place thumb and middle finger against chest and move them away from body, touching tips.

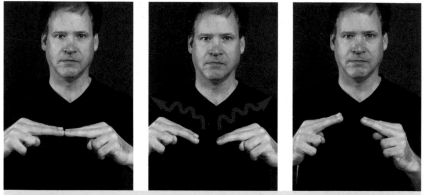

BACON

"H" sign both hands, palms down, tips touching. Move apart in a wavy motion.

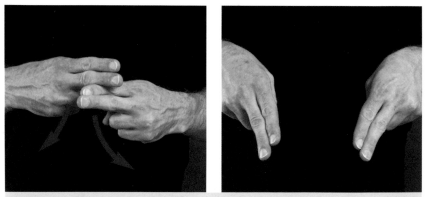

EGGS

"H" sign both hands, palms in. Hit L "H" sign with R and then draw apart as if cracking an egg.

FOR
Touch forehead with R index finger. Turn outward and move forward.

BREAKFAST
Tap R "O" to mouth.

Place fingertips of R hand in crook of L arm. Raise L arm to vertical position.

She wants chocolate ice cream.

SHE
Draw a line down side of cheek with thumb of R "A" and then point.

WANTS
"5" hands, palms up, fingers curved. Draw toward body.

CHOCOLATE
Place thumb of R "C" on back of L hand and circle in a counterclockwise motion.

ICE CREAM
"S" sign at chin, move down twice, miming licking an ice-cream cone.

I want salt and pepper, please.

I
Place R "I" against chest.

WANT
"5" hands, palms up, fingers curved. Draw toward body.

SALT
Tap R "V" on back of L "V" several times.

PEPPER
Shake R "O" up and down as if sprinkling pepper.

PLEASE
Rub R palm in circle on chest.

Give the poor man a glass of milk.

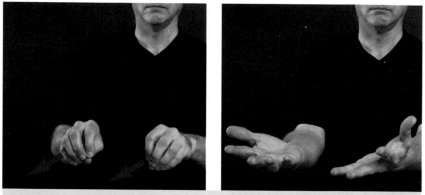

GIVE

"O" sign both hands, palms down, L slightly ahead of R. Move forward, opening fingers.

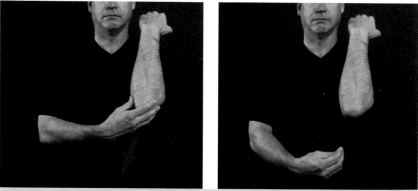

POOR

Place open R hand over L elbow and pull down twice, closing fingers at end of motion.

GLASS
L palm up, place R "C" onto L palm and raise up to indicate a tall glass.

MAN
Mime grabbing brim of hat with R forefingers and thumb.

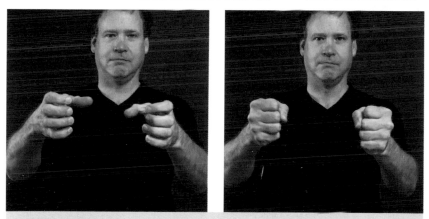

MILK
Open and close "S" sign both hands, knuckles in. Mime milking a cow.

Cut the meat with your knife and fork.

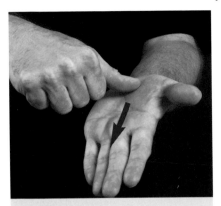

CUT
Move thumb of R "A" sign across upturned L palm.

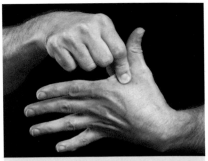

MEAT
L hand palm in, tips R. Touch flesh between L thumb and index finger with R thumb and index finger.

WITH
Place "A" hands together, palm to palm.

YOUR
Point R palm at subject.

KNIFE
Slide tips of R "U" against tip of L index finger and repeat.

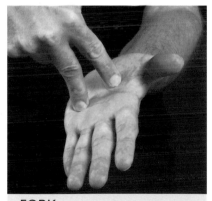

FORK
L hand palm up, tips R. Tap L palm with tips of R "V."

We grow peas, carrots, and onions in the garden.

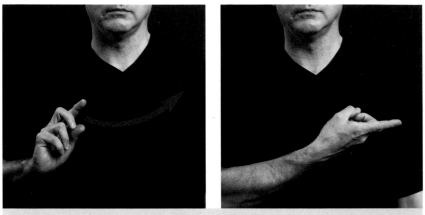

WE
Place R index finger at R shoulder and circle around to L shoulder.

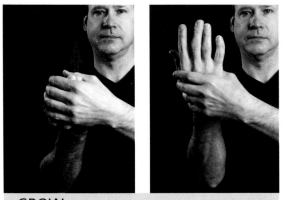

GROW
R "O" hand opens as it passes through L "C," both palms facing body.

PEAS
"1" sign with L hand, palm in, tip R. Tap along finger from base to tip with R "X."

CARROTS
Hold R "S" sign up to mouth and twist slightly as if eating a carrot.

ONIONS
Twist R "X" sign at the corner of R eye.

IN
Place R fingertips into L "C."

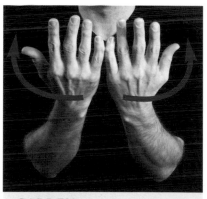

GARDEN
Rotate hands from in front of chest to the side in a semicircle.

Do you take sugar in tea?

YOU
Point R index finger at subject.

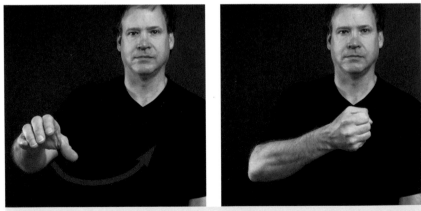

TAKE
Draw R hand from L to R, ending in an "S."

SUGAR
R "H" sign, palm in. Stroke fingertips down chin twice.

IN
Place R fingertips into L "C."

TEA
Place thumb and index finger of R "F" sign into L "O" sign and stir.

?
Form question mark in the air with R index finger.

HE

Mime grabbing brim of hat, then point R index finger at subject.

DRINK
With R "C," hold an imaginary glass and tip toward mouth.

WINE
R "W" sign, palm L. Circle at R cheek.

?
Form question mark in the air with R index finger.

I like a cheese sandwich for lunch.

I
Place R "I" against chest.

LIKE
Place thumb and middle finger against chest and move them away from body, touching tips.

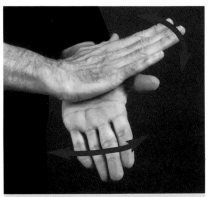

CHEESE
Twist heels of both palms together.

SANDWICH
Palms together, bring hands toward mouth.

FOR
Touch forehead with R index finger and turn outward and forward.

LUNCH
Tap the fingertips of the R "O" on the mouth several times.

Bend the L arm in front of the body, pointing R. R elbow on L fingertips, arm vertical, palm in.

On the Move

EXPENSIVE
Place R "O" on L palm. Lift R hand and draw it away, opening slightly.

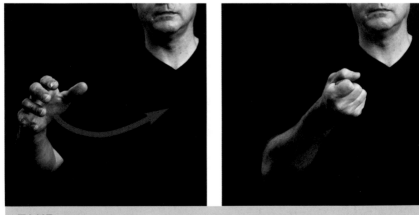

TAKE
Draw R "5" from L to R, ending in an "S."

AIRPLANE
R "Y" sign with index finger extended. Move away from body.

AROUND
With R index finger, draw circle around upturned tips of L "O."

WORLD
"W" sign both hands, tips out. Place R "W" on top of L, then circle R "W" around L and return to original position.

?
Form question mark in the air with R index finger.

I rode my bicycle from home to the library.

I
Place R "I" against chest.

RODE
Place curved R "U" in L "C" and move forward.

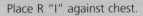

MY
R palm flat on chest.

BICYCLE
"S" sign both hands, knuckles down, L hand below R. Make pedaling motion with hands.

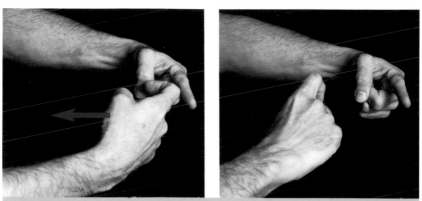

FROM

L index finger pointing R, palm in. R "X" against L index finger, palm L. Pull R "X" toward body.

HOME

Place tips of R "O" sign on R edge of mouth and move to the R cheek.

LIBRARY

R "L" sign, palm out, move in a circle.

How much does it cost on the train across Canada?

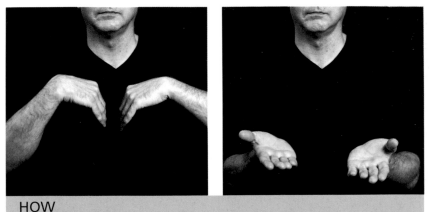

HOW
Place backs of hands together, fingers down. Rotate away from body, ending with palms up in front of body.

MUCH
Hands in front of body, palms facing, fingers spread and slightly bent. Separate hands.

COST
L palm R, tips out. Brush R "X" sign down L palm.

TRAIN
"H" sign both hands, palms down, L tips R, R tips L. Rub R "H" back and forth on L "H."

ON
Place R palm on back of L hand.

ACROSS
L hand palm down, tips R. R hand tips out, palm L, slide forward across back of L hand.

CANADA
Grab and shake R side of shirt with R hand.

?
Form question mark in the air with R index finger.

Did the car turn left into the school?

CAR
"S" sign both hands, palms facing, mime turning a steering wheel.

TURN
With L index finger pointed up, palm in, rotate R index finger around L.

LEFT
R "L" sign, palm out. Move from R to L.

INTO
Place R fingertips into L "C."

SCHOOL
L palm up, tips out. R hand down, tips L. Clap hands.

?
Form question mark in the air with R index finger.

The ambulance was behind the truck and the motorcycle.

AMBULANCE
R "A" sign, make a cross on upper L arm.

WAS
Move R "W" sign back, ending in an "S."

BEHIND

"A" sign both hands, knuckles facing, thumbs up. Place hands together and draw R hand back.

TRUCK

"S" sign both hands, palms facing. Mime holding and moving a large steering wheel.

MOTORCYCLE

"S" sign both hands in front of body as if grasping handlebars. Twist inward twice.

On Wednesday I took the bus to the store.

ON
Place R palm on back of L hand.

WEDNESDAY
Circle R "W," palm out.

I
Place R "I" against chest.

TOOK
Draw R hand from L to R, ending in an "S."

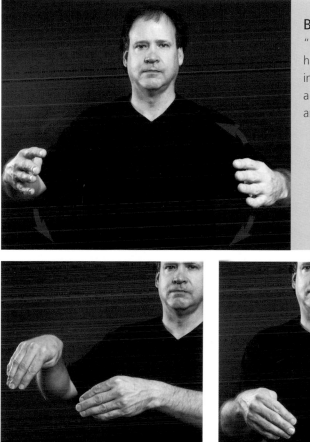

BUS

"B" sign both hands, palms facing. Mime holding a steering wheel and turning.

STORE

"O" sign both hands, tips down. Swing out twice.

On Saturday we drove to the restaurant.

ON
Place R palm on back of L hand.

SATURDAY
R "S," palm out. Rotate.

WE
Place R index finger at R shoulder and circle around to L shoulder.

DROVE
"S" sign both hands, move as if turning a car's steering wheel.

RESTAURANT
R "R" sign, palm L. Place on R side of mouth, then move to L side.

The boat goes between England and America.

BOAT

Both hands palms up, slightly cupped, little fingers touching. Move forward twice.

GOES

"1" sign both hands, palms in. Rotate hands around each other, moving away from body.

BETWEEN

L hand palm in and tips R. With R hand palm L and tips out, slide back and forth on the L index finger.

ENGLAND

Hold L wrist with R hand and move forward and back.

AMERICA

Interlock fingers of both hands and circle in front of body from R to L.

My house is behind the post office.

MY
R palm flat on chest.

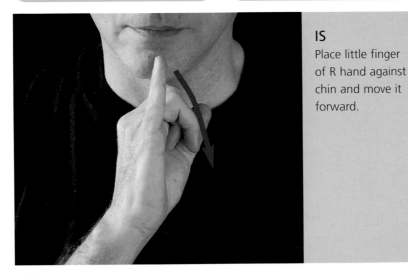

HOUSE
Place tips of both hands together to form a roof, then move apart and down to form the sides of the house.

IS
Place little finger of R hand against chin and move it forward.

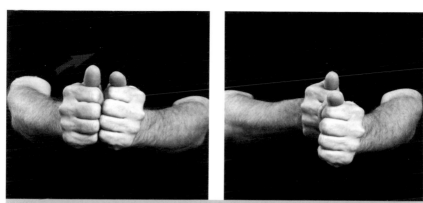

BEHIND

"A" sign both hands, knuckles facing, thumbs up. Place hands together and draw R hand back.

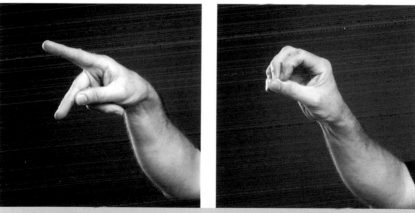

POST OFFICE

Finger spell "P" and "O."

In which months is the college open?

IN
Place R fingertips into L "C."

WHICH
With both "A" hands in front of body, raise and lower alternately, palms facing.

MONTH
"1" sign both hands, L palm R, R palm in, tip L. Place R index finger against L index finger and slide down.

IS
Place little finger of R hand against chin and move it forward.

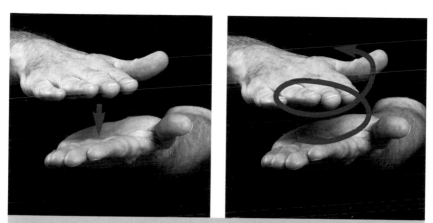

COLLEGE
Clap hands together once and circle R hand upward over L palm.

OPEN
R and L "B" hands, palms out and index fingers touching, draw apart, ending with palms facing.

?
Form question mark in the air with R index finger.

245

The movie costs five dollars and fifty cents.

MOVIE

"5" sign both hands, L palm tips out. R hand palm L, tips up. Place palms together and shake R tips back and forth to indicate a flickering motion.

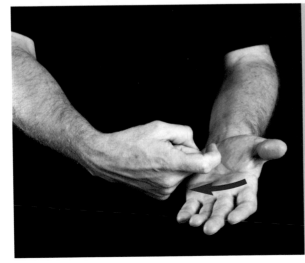

COSTS

L hand palm R, tips out. Brush R "X" sign down L palm.

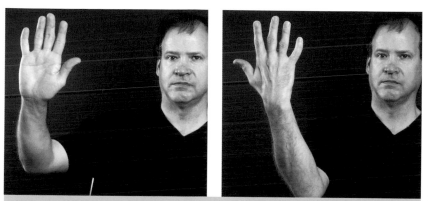

FIVE DOLLARS

Hold up number "5," palm forward. Turn wrist around and up, finishing with palm in.

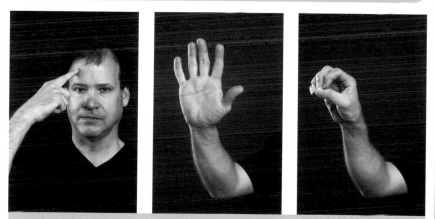

FIFTY CENTS

Touch R index finger to forehead, then sign "5" and "0."

In which country do you live?

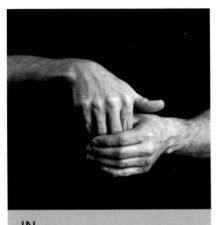

IN
Place R fingertips into L "C."

WHICH
With both "A" hands in front of body, raise and lower alternately, palms facing.

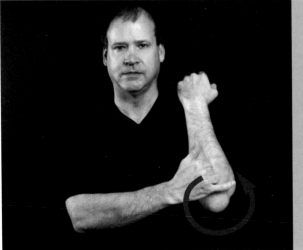

COUNTRY
Rub L elbow clockwise with R "Y" sign.

YOU
Point R index finger at subject.

LIVE
Both "L" signs, palms in, brush up the chest.

?
Form question mark in the air with R index finger.

It is warm in summer.

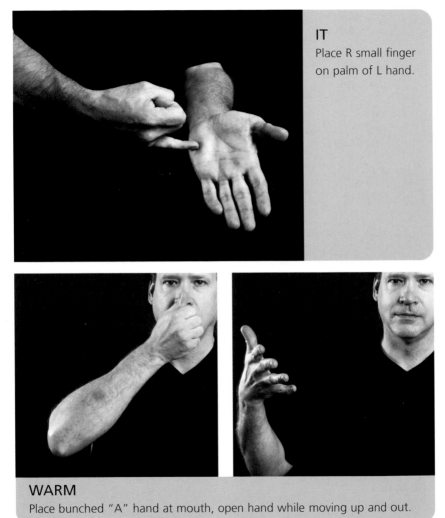

IT
Place R small finger on palm of L hand.

WARM
Place bunched "A" hand at mouth, open hand while moving up and out.

IN
Place R fingertips into L "C."

SUMMER
R "D" sign on forehead, tip L, rub L to R across forehead, ending with an "X" sign.

Go right, then go through.

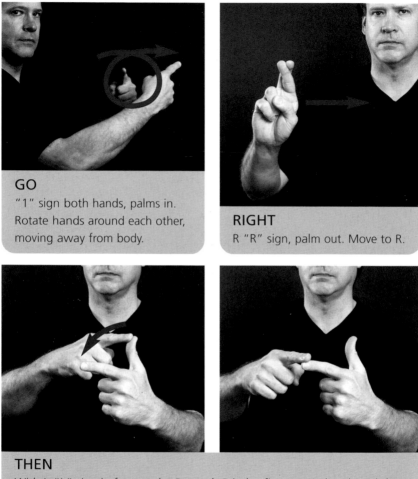

GO
"1" sign both hands, palms in. Rotate hands around each other, moving away from body.

RIGHT
R "R" sign, palm out. Move to R.

THEN
With L "L" sign in front, palm R, touch R index finger to L thumb and then to L index finger.

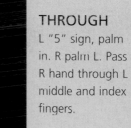

GO
"1" sign both hands, palms in. Rotate hands around each other, moving away from body.

THROUGH
L "5" sign, palm in. R palm L. Pass R hand through L middle and index fingers.

Index